*This book is dedicated to the Holy Spirit,
The Helper of my soul
And the One behind all the
revelations shared in this book.
To Him alone be glory, honor, and power
Forever and ever, amen.*

He has come that you may have life, *and that
you may have it more* abundantly. *(John 10:10b)*

DEMONIC MANIPULATION IN DREAMS

Rev. James Solomon

ISBN 979-8-88832-754-8 (paperback)
ISBN 979-8-88832-755-5 (digital)

Copyright © 2024 by Rev. James Solomon

All rights reserved. No part of this publication may be reproduced, distributed, or transmitted in any form or by any means, including photocopying, recording, or other electronic or mechanical methods without the prior written permission of the publisher. For permission requests, solicit the publisher via the address below.

Christian Faith Publishing
832 Park Avenue
Meadville, PA 16335
www.christianfaithpublishing.com

Printed in the United States of America

CONTENTS

Acknowledgment vii
Chapter 1   Demonic Manipulation in Your Dreams 1
Chapter 2   Dreams from God 7
Chapter 3   The Seed of the Enemy 15
Chapter 4   The Diverse Nature of Manipulations 21
Chapter 5   Why Do Demons Manipulate Our Dreams? 25
Chapter 6   Some Common Dream Patterns................................30
Chapter 7   Warfare Prayers against Dream Manipulations 36
    i.   Prayer of preparation before deliverance 36
    ii. Scriptures for deliverance and spiritual warfare.........37
    iii. Repentance and confession..40
    iv. Breaking evil covenants and curses from the bloodline! 42
    v.   Prayers against the manipulation of witchcraft and familiar spirits 48
    vi. Deliverance from spirit husband or wife...................50
    vii. Prayers against dream manipulations 52
    viii. Scriptural declaration of victory through the blood of Jesus 56

ACKNOWLEDGMENT

Discovering the importance of people in the pursuit of greatness is one of the best discoveries we can make in life. It is important to note that from the cradle to the grave, we will always need people who will help us to succeed and fulfill our divine destiny.

I want to express my appreciation to some people whom God has placed in my life to assist me in my journey toward greatness. This book is a joint effort of people who have believed in my vision and have contributed immensely in one area or the other to make it a reality.

I want to thank my father in the Lord, the late Rev. Dr. James Boyejo. Your life and ministry have greatly impacted my life for good, and I just can't forget you, sir. Pastor Enoch Adeboye, the general overseer of the Redeemed Christian Church of God (worldwide), is my mentor whose life and ministry have been a perfect example to me at all times. Sir, I love and appreciate the opportunity given to me to be a blessing to the body of Christ in the Redeemed Christian Church of God (worldwide). Thanks a lot for always being there for me.

I would like to express my appreciation to my faithful friends—Rev. Kayode Kolawole of Power House of Jesus Ministries, Ibadan (Nigeria); Evangelist Mike Okuo, AIG (retired), who is always a source of encouragement to me; and to my special friend Rev. Dr. Omomokuyo of Christ Anointed Kingdom Church, Lagos (Nigeria).

A big thanks to all my faithful pastors who are committed to the vision of Jesus People's Revival Ministries and Jesus Family Chapel in Nigeria, Kenya, Sierra Leone, and the United States of America.

CHAPTER 1

Demonic Manipulation in Your Dreams

Heavenly Father, we thank You for Your faithfulness. You are the only One that has answers and solutions to all our questions. We ask that You reveal Your mind to us on this subject so that Your purpose alone will be established in the church, and Your people will receive the truth directly from You; and after reading this book, everyone will have victory over Satan's manipulations. Thank You, Lord, for answering our prayers. For we have prayed in Jesus's name. Amen.

This subject is very multifaceted with people going as far as selling books entitled *How to Interpret Your Dreams*. Some people under the influence of the occult try to interpret and read meanings into dreams, which in turn have affected many people negatively. Dreams were instituted by God and, therefore, are scriptural. Many people argue about the importance of dreams in our lives, but it is my hope that after reading this book, you will have a clear understanding on this topic.

Reading the Bible from Genesis to Revelation will confirm that dreams have a scriptural foundation. It was through dreams that God rescued the baby Jesus from the hands of King Herod. People ignore their dreams because they fail to realize that dreams are scriptural and need to be studied and prayed upon. People condemn and/or forget their dreams because they do not understand the importance of it.

According to dictionary definition, dreams are "nightmares, visions, fantasies, aspirations, trances," and so on. The secular world defines dreams as they understand it because they do not have a proper knowledge or understanding of the Word of God. Therefore, what is the true definition of dreams from a biblical point of view? God is the Creator of all living things on earth, and so it goes without saying that He alone can give the proper definition, explanation, and/or details of what dreams are. God sometimes uses dreams to guide us or reveal the solutions to various problems; however, we should also be aware that some dreams also come from Satan, who always strives to make a counterfeit of all that God has and does.

> For God speaketh once, yea twice, yet man perceiveth it not. In a dream, in a vision of the night, when deep sleep falleth upon men, in slumberings upon the bed; Then he openeth the ears of men, and sealeth their instruction. That he may withdraw man from his purpose, and hide pride from man. He keepeth back his soul from the pit, and his life from perishing by the sword. (Job 33:14–18)

From this passage, we see that God uses dreams to explain deep spiritual truths that we would not perceive or understand in the natural. If we are to be honest with ourselves, a lot of us do not allow God to speak to us (because of one reason or the other), or when He does speaks, we don't recognize His voice.

It is also clear from this passage that dreams take place when one is in a deep sleep. If one falls asleep in the middle of a sermon during a church service, he might fall into a trance, but he will most definitely not be dreaming. Dreams are usually attached to a deep sleep.

> In order to turn man from his deed, and conceal pride from man. (Job 33:17 NKJ)

This is one of the purposes of dreams. How many times have you woken up from your sleep after a dream and immediately began to pray because of the feelings that particular dreams stirred up in you (like fear, reverence, confusion, etc.)? Have you ever had an out-of-body experience in your dreams in which you were watching yourself doing certain things or performing certain actions? I have heard of cases in which people find themselves watching their own funeral in their dreams. They see themselves being laid out in the casket with people mourning, grieving, and crying all around. Such dreams are ways God show us that we are not just physical human beings, but we are also spirit beings.

Joseph, the husband of Mary (the mother of Jesus), had no intention of traveling at a certain point in time. His original plan probably was to settle down and establish himself in the town where he was, but having received instructions from the angel (regarding the threat on the life of Jesus) in his dream, he woke up immediately and took both mother and child and departed to the place God told him. So we see that God sometimes uses dreams to reveal His plans and purpose for our lives, which usually supersedes whatever plans we could have. Again, dreams are scriptural.

At this point, I will like to state that there are people who do not dream at all, while others dream, and as soon as they wake up, they forget the dream. These are satanic manipulations. Not only are human beings supposed to have dreams, but also we are expected to remember whatever we dreamt about. Forgetting one's dream is a witchcraft or demonic operation; their duty is to erase the dreams for your memory so that you will not receive whatever revelation the Lord is giving to you. Assuming you receive a revelation in your dream that will lead to a major breakthrough in your life, or let's assume that in your dream, God reveals the plans and activities of the enemy against your life, the kingdom of darkness will not want you to know or remember these dreams because you will obviously pray about them and seek spiritual help. And so the enemy (Satan and his demons) will try by all means to wipe out your dreams from memory. One of the most powerful weapons of the kingdom of darkness is forgetfulness. These satanic manipulations will be properly addressed in this book, and at the end, I believe that you will have your deliverance and be free.

Do not make the mistake of thinking that all dreams are demonic. When reading the Bible, you will find out that many times, God revealed Himself to men through dreams. He also gave several warnings, instructions, and so on through dreams. In many passages of the Bible, it is clear that God uses dreams as a means of communication.

> He keepeth back his soul from the pit, and his life from perishing by the sword. (Job 33:18)

The dream life is very important. It is sometimes difficult for God to get our full and undivided attention even during prayers, and so He uses dreams to guide us and direct our steps to His perfect will.

> For a dream cometh through the multitude of business; and a fool's voice is known by multitude of words. (Ecclesiastes 5:3)

Dreams come from three major sources:

1. *From God (Job 33:14)*
2. *From a multitude of business (in the mind) (Ecclesiastes 5:3).* These are dreams that come from the anxieties, sorrows, problems, and/or thoughts that we face every day. Let's take an unmarried lady for example, who spends all her time, night and day, praying to God for a husband. When she sleeps at night, she is more than likely going to dream about herself being married. She might see herself at the altar getting married.
3. *From the devil (Matthew 13:25)*

> But while men slept, his enemy came and sowed tares among the wheat, and went his way. (Matthew 13:25)

This is type of dream is a satanic manipulation, but I believe that the Lord God Almighty will enlighten us on how to handle this problem.

The human being consists of a spirit, soul, and a body. A man's achievements in life depend largely on his spirit being, which is why it is very important to guard our spirits and watch what goes into our spirit being. We are spirit beings born of the Holy Spirit, and so our destinies are issued in the spiritual realm. In other words, the only way to get to our destiny is through our spirit. A lot of people are not successful today because their destinies have been destroyed in the spirit realm, and even though they battle and struggle in the physical, there seems to be little next to no change in their lives. As you read this book, I pray that the Almighty God in His mercies and power will flush out every seed that the devil has succeeded in planting into our lives in the name of Jesus!

There was once a Muslim lady who dreamt that a crown was stolen away from her head by some men dressed in black. Two years later, someone invited this lady to a revival meeting where I was ministering. During the prayer time, she fell under the anointing of the Holy Spirit. When she came to, she said she saw five men dressed in white bringing back the crown that was stolen from her. Brethren, do not take your dreams for granted.

Make this confession out loud: "I *shall be totally delivered today* in the name of Jesus!"

God might have endowed you with excellent potentials in life, but it is also possible for the forces of darkness to steal away your destiny through your dreams. Most times in the lives of believers, the enemy is able to plant these seeds (of destruction) because there are loopholes or open doors in their lives as a result of sin. There was once a brother who was continuously warned by the Lord about a certain thing, but he refused to yield to the warning. One night while he slept, the devil struck him with epilepsy. The devil is watching out for the loopholes in your lives. Be careful!

The bottom line of this study is that dreams are scriptural. As a child of God, you have every right and the liberty to uproot all evil seeds the devil might have planted in your life through dreams.

Make this confession out loud: "*I shall uproot!*"

> But he answered and said, Every plant, which my heavenly Father hath not planted, shall be rooted up. (Matthew 15:13)

A woman once was brought to me who had breast cancer. Her condition was so bad that both her breasts smelled and were almost disfigured; she had to wear about three or four layers of clothing just to try to hide the offensive odor. She had visited several hospitals, but the more medication and treatment she received, the worse her condition became.

During my talk with this woman, I asked her about her dreams. She told me that before she became ill, she had a dream in which someone shot an arrow at her left breast. When she woke up, she felt pain in her left breast, but the people around her advised her to dismiss the dream and what she felt. Two years later, the pain in her left breast increased and became very painful to the point that the breast could not be saved. A few more years after, both breasts became infected. At this point, the medical doctors wanted to perform a surgical operation on her, but they were not sure she would survive the procedure. It was at this stage she was brought to me. Alas! It was too little too late! Why was it too late? She failed to pray or do anything at the initial stage when she first had the dream. She died a few days later. You have to be mindful and careful about your dreams.

In another example, a woman was given a delicious meal in her dream which she ate. When she woke up, her hands were shaking. Three years later, both her hands and feet were numb and completely unresponsive, and this was when she was brought to me. Again, dreams are real, and both God and Satan use dreams.

CHAPTER 2

Dreams from God

When our bodies and minds are resting, our spirits become more alert and apt to receive, and that is why God sometimes communicates to us through dreams. In the Bible, we see that Joseph's destiny was revealed in full detail through his dreams. King Solomon also received revelations of wisdom, glory, and wealth in his dreams. Therefore, God can reveal your destiny to you through your dreams. This method of revelation is the easiest method through which God communicates with us, and it does not require much effort on our part. All we need to do is sleep. However, in order to have a clean dream, we must have a clean spirit.

Most dreams that we sometimes consider to be bad may not necessarily be bad; they might be a symbolic form of the will of God. If like the Pharaoh of Egypt you had a dream in which seven thin and ugly cows were eating up seven fat and good looking cows, would you not wake up immediately and begin to bind and rebuke the devil? After all, such a dream cannot be from God. As we continue in this study, we will be able to determine the source of our dreams.

I urge you to stop seeking for interpretation of dreams from books that supposedly interpret dreams. The interpretation of dreams comes from God *alone*, and so He is the *only* One we should turn to. One reason why reading books such as *The ABC of Interpreting Dreams* is not a good idea is that the interpretation such books may give to a particular dream may by completely different from the interpretation given by God, and this could end up being very dangerous.

While I was preaching on this topic in a church in London, there was a young lady and her mother present in the congregation. At the end of my sermon, the mother urged her to come to me and request for prayers because she never dreams whenever she sleeps. I prayed for her and that very night the lady had a dream in which the Lord revealed all the deep secrets about her family to her. Remember, it is not good not to have dreams, just as it is not a good thing to have a dream and forget it; these are signs of witchcraft activities. For the Pharaoh of Egypt (in the time of Joseph), the devil's plan was to wipe out the revelation that God gave him his dreams concerning the future of Egypt. Imagine what would have happened if Pharaoh forgot the dreams he had or if there was no Joseph to interpret Pharaoh's dreams. The consequences would have been disastrous as a whole nation would have faced untold torment, agony, and hardship for years. This is exactly what the enemy wants to accomplish in your life (chaos and hardship), so you have to be willing and ready to wage war and fight these battles against the enemy.

God uses dreams for many reasons, one of which is to warn us about an impending calamity or doom (plans of the enemy). Forgetting one's dream, therefore, is not an option, and if you do forget your dreams, you need to ask God for the power and ability to always remember your dreams. It is very important and essential for you to know what messages or instructions the Lord is passing across to you through your dreams; this cannot be overemphasized. After praying, I assure you that you will begin to receive deep revelations in your dreams.

Blind men and women do have dreams, so this is a proof that dreams are spiritual. Many Christians today need a spiritual "tune up." Therefore, we need to ask the Lord to clean out our entire system. Let us take a look at some scriptures that will convince us beyond a shadow of a doubt that we are entitled to have dreams. The ability to dream is one of the main differences between an animal and a human being.

> But God came to Abimelech *in a dream by night*, and said to him, Behold, thou art but a

dead man, for the woman which thou hast taken;
for she is a man's wife. (Genesis 20:3)

For those of you who do not dream, the Lord will touch (and heal) your system. This day, the Holy Spirit will clean up your retentive memory. Don't you realize that there are precious revelations that the Lord wants to give you concerning your future? Before I became a Christian, I felt I was not entitled to dreams because I could not remember my dreams. I knew I had dreams while I slept, but once I was awake, I would forget them. There were times I sensed that I dreamt about something very important, but I would forget about it, and there was nothing I could do to remedy the situation. Now I know that whatever the case maybe, you can pray that the power of God will consume every force blindfolding you in the name of Jesus. Abimelech was an "unbeliever," yet when he slept, he dreamt and received a warning from God. How much more a believer? Shouldn't a believer receive revelations from God?

There are some people that dream and never forget their dreams, yet most of the time, their dreams come to pass in a negative form. For instance, if a man sees himself riding a car in a dream, it is an indication that he will lose the car he owns. Or if someone dreams about the birth of a baby, they automatically know that someone is about to die. These dreams are examples of satanic manipulation, satanic forces that reverse dreams. There is a clear difference between symbolic or allegorical dreams and negative dreams. God can give a dream that represents something He wants to express; this is completely different from having a beautiful dream reversed in physical life or reality. Sometimes, God can give a dream that needs no interpretation for it to be understood. At other times, He can also give a dream that requires interpretation, which is why we need to pray to God for the interpretation of dreams.

And being warned of God in a dream that they should not return to Herod, they departed into their own country another way. (Matthew 2:12)

Can you imagine what would have happened if the three wise men forgot the dream they had? A lot of problems and unnecessary hardship are usually the results of a forgotten dream. Many revelations, solutions, and warnings have been lost because certain dreams were forgotten. A Christian brother once received a warning in a dream that he should not drive his car for a whole day; it was on a Sunday. He obeyed the instruction given to him in the dream and had someone else give him a ride to church. At the end of the church service, the brother's housemaid came up to him and asked who informed him not to drive his car on that particular day because in their gathering of witches, they had decided that he would die in a car accident on that day. She brought a medium-size container that supposedly contained engine oil and showed it to the brother, saying it contained his blood that had mystically been drained out of him and that there was no way to put the blood back into his body. The brother was speechless and sent for the pastor of the church to inform him of what was happening. Obviously—and thank God—nothing happened to the brother; but suppose he did not yield to the warning given in his dream or he forgot his dream, the plans of the witches would have come to pass. You may not be anointed to preach or perform miracles, but at least you should have dreams at night when you sleep.

> And when they were departed, behold, the angel of the Lord appeareth to Joseph in a dream saying, Arise, and take the young child and his mother, and flee into Egypt, and be thou there until I bring thee word: for Herod will seek the young child to destroy him. (Matthew 2:13)

Again, let's assume that Joseph woke up and forgot the dream he had or maybe he remembered but decided to ignore the warning, can you imagine the consequence? Dreaming is scriptural. Anyone can directly hear and know the mind of God through dreams. I encourage you to begin to desire and long for revelations through dreams. Many do not know the importance, and this is why the enemy is able to infiltrate their lives. It is your right as a child of God to request a revelation about your daily affairs in (or through) your dreams. Do not always depend of men of God or prophets.

There was a time I went to pray on a mountain. In the country where I come from (Nigeria, West Africa), there are facilities in some mountains that are designated for prayers. As I went there to spend some time fasting and praying, a lady was brought to the mountain. She was suffering from a hopeless case of tuberculosis. As soon as I saw her, the Holy Spirit asked me to pray for her. I approached her, laid my hands on her, and prayed for her. After praying for her, her condition seemed to get worse, but while she slept that night, she had a dream. In the dream, she saw a doctor dressed in white, performing a surgery on her. He removed a dark substance from her stomach and showed it to her as the cause of her sickness. When she woke up, she was completely healed. This is a true illustration that shows that God can remove demonic deposits from our bodies even in our dreams.

A few years ago, I established my ministry in a particular part of Nigeria (which is in West Africa). A while later, I had a dream about a lady whose, whenever she stretches her hand, hair on one side of my head will fall off. In that same dream, I took authority and dominion in the name of Jesus and recovered all my hair. When I woke up, I understood how dangerous that mission field (where I established my ministry) could be, and I became more diligent and determined. To the glory of God, we got the victory, and the ministry was (and still is) successful.

God uses dreams, thus making them very important. God used dreams to exalt Joseph to the position of prime minister of the greatest nation of his time.

> And Joseph dreamed a dream, and he told it his brethren: and they hated him yet the more. And he said unto them, Hear, I pray you, this dream which I have dreamed: For, behold, we were binding sheaves in the field, and, lo, my sheaf arose and also stood upright; and, behold, your sheaves stood round about, and made

> obeisance to my sheaf. And his brethren said to him, Shalt thou indeed reign over us? Or shalt thou indeed have dominion over us? And they hated him yet the more for his dreams, and for his words. And he dreamed yet another dream, and told it his brethren, and said, Behold, I have dreamed a dream more; and, behold, the sun and the moon and the eleven stars made obeisance to me. And he told it to his father, and to his brethren: and his father rebuked him, and said unto him, What is this dream that thou hast dreamed? Shall I and thy mother and thy brethren indeed come to bow down ourselves to thee to the earth? (Genesis 37:5–10)

This is the revelation God gave Joseph in a dream about his future. At that time, he did not have any Bible verse to back it up, nor did he have the Law of Moses, yet the dream came to pass. From today, I challenge you to be more opened to the revelation God may pass across to you through your dreams. It is not every dream that should be ignored or rejected, and not every dream is demonic. The devil has ways of manipulating God's revelations in your dreams, but we will consider that in a later chapter.

> And he dreamed, and behold a ladder set up on the earth, and the top of it reached to heaven: and behold the angels of God ascending and descending on it. And, behold, the Lord stood above it, and said, I am the Lord God of Abraham thy father, and the Isaac: the land whereon thou liest, to thee will I give it, and to thy seed; And thy seed shall be as the dust of the earth, and thou shalt spread abroad to the west, and to the east, and to the north, and to the south: and in thee and in thy seed shall all the families of the earth be blessed. And behold, I am with thee, and

will keep thee in all places wither thou goest, and will bring thee again into this land; for I will not leave thee, until I have done that which I have spoken to thee of. And Jacob awaked out of his sleep, and he said, Surely the Lord is in this place; and I knew it not. (Genesis 28:12–16)

This is another scripture that proves that God speaks to us through dreams. Besides giving clear warnings in our dreams, God also reveals His plans for greatness in our dreams.

And he said, Hear now my words: If there be a prophet among you, I the Lord will make myself known unto him in a vision, and will speak unto him in a dream. (Numbers 12:6)

The prophet that hath a dream, let him tell a dream; and he that hath my word, let him speak my word faithfully. What is the chaff to the wheat? Saith the Lord. (Jeremiah 23:28)

While I was in fasting and prayers on the prayer mountain, a Christian brother came up to the same mountain. He was a business man who owned a number of stores which all ran out of business within a short period of time. On a particular night, I was asked to lead the prayer session. At 2:00 a.m., after the prayers, we all went to sleep. One hour later, this brother came running to me and woke me up. He said he had a dream in which he saw a man and a lady; the lady was the owner of the store located opposite one of his stores. He explained that this lady had once taken him to see a voodoo (occult) priest to make some charms for his business to run smoothly and successfully. This priest is the man he saw in his dream. In this dream, the priest informed him that the lady was the reason behind his failing stores and business. The lady had tricked him into turning his business over to the voodoo priest for evil purposes while pretending to help him protect and secure his business.

After narrating his dream to me, I prayed and asked God to continue the dream so that the brother would find a way to recover his business. When we finished praying, the brother slept, and the dream continued. This time, in the dream, the brother took authority and dominion over the voodoo priest and commanded him to release of all of his goods and businesses in his possession in Jesus's name. From that moment, the brother's once-failing business turned around, and he began to prosper again.

Make this confession out loud:

> Lord, release your satellite into my system today. Remove every covering that prevents me from dreaming and receiving your revelation in the name of Jesus! Holy Ghost fire, consume all the forces that swallow up my dreams from God and their manifestations in the name of Jesus! I am secured in the power that resurrected Jesus Christ from death. I condemn every spiritual manipulation, blindness, coverings, and veils that are preventing me from receiving revelations from God in my dreams. Holy Ghost, by fire open my inner eyes and ears now in the name of Jesus!

CHAPTER 3

The Seed of the Enemy

> Another parable put he forth unto them, saying, The kingdom of heaven is likened unto a man which sowed good seed in his field: But while men slept, his enemy came and sowed tares among the wheat, and went his way. But when the blade was sprung up, and brought forth fruit, then appeared the tares also. So the servants of the householder came and said unto him, Sir, didst not thou sow good see in thy field? From whence then hath it tares? He said unto them, An enemy hath done this. (Matthew13:24–28a)

There is a difference between parables and fables. A fable is a story which is unreal and is often personified with animal characters; it is usually intended to convey a moral truth. A parable on the other hand is a story or allegory with a moral to it. Jesus used this parable above to explain the kingdom of God as an abstract concept. The following is the explanation Jesus was trying to convey through this parable:

> He answered, "The one who sowed the good seed is the Son of Man. The field is the world, and the good seed stands for the people of the kingdom. The weeds are the people of the evil one, And the enemy who sows them is the

devil. The harvest is the end of the age, and the harvesters are angels. As the weeds are pulled up and burned in the fire, so it will be at the end of the age. The Son of Man will send out His angels, and they will weed out of His kingdom everything that causes sin and all who do evil. They will throw them into the blazing furnace, where there will be weeping and gnashing of teeth. Then the righteous will shine like the sun in the kingdom of their Father. Whoever has ears, let them hear. (Matthew 13:37–43)

From this parable and its interpretation, we understand that the *good seeds* are the children of God, and the *bad seeds* are the wicked ones from the devil. We can also say that we (the believers) are the *good seeds* of the earth.

Another analogy that can be deduced from this parable is that God created us with tremendous potentials and a perfect destiny. We are the seeds of God, and everything He planted is a good seed. Having a job, being in good health, or being married does not determine the quality of a seed. If the seed is from God, it is good! Believers need to know that they were not created from bad seeds, but they were created with a high potential of success. Our physical, financial, material, or spiritual state does not change the fact that God says we are good seeds.

There was once a young teenager who had a promising future; his parents were very proud of him and his achievements. Suddenly, he was very ill and eventually became paralyzed. His parents took him to all the doctors, hospitals, and anointed men of God for healing, yet to no avail. One day, the young boy requested that one of his pictures should be enlarged and placed in his bedroom. He then began to pray asking God to restore him and his health back to the way he was in his younger days as seen in the enlarged picture. What he was requesting unconsciously was that God should restore the original good seed He had planted. He understood that from his beginning, he was a good seed, and he wanted to be restored back to that beginning. After making this request before God several times, the boy received his complete healing, and just like this young boy, you will be restored back to *the original you*! Whatever the devil has sown in your life—bareness, poverty, sorrow, depression, or bad health—it is time to for you to be restored back to your original position. Jesus has declared "you are a good seed." Whenever you are challenged with difficulties of any kind, remember His words.

Make this confession out loud: *"I am going back to the original me."*

Some people foolishly argue that the devil cannot harm any child of God, but the Bible says, "While men slept." In other words, the devil is looking for a time of inattention. From a spiritual stand point, the night is regarded as a very sensitive time. Throughout the New Testament, Jesus refers to the night as a time when no man works. In other words, it is a time when no man watches:

> As long as it is day, we must do the works of him who sent me. Night is coming, when no one can work. (John 9:4 NIV)

Therefore, it is always good to say a word of prayer before sleeping, for the enemy is watching for any opening—even through dreams. It is very important for us to live a victorious Christian life in the physical. In that way, we will be victorious in our dreams. However, if our Christian walk is physically weak, we will not also have victory in our dreams. So make it a point of duty to build up your spirit in the Lord; this is the only way you can have dreams free from evil seeds.

> But ye, beloved, building up yourselves on your most holy faith, praying in the Holy Ghost. (Jude 1:20)

The first gateway to demons and evil seeds is a sinful life. People who are possessed or oppressed by demons can be freed with a prayer of deliverance, but that prayer becomes powerless if that person goes back to his or her sinful life. As a matter of fact, the Bible says such a person has opened the door to seven stronger demons:

> When the unclean spirit is gone out of a man, he walketh through dry places, seeking rest, and findeth none. Then he saith, "I will return into my house from whence I came out"; and when he is come, he findeth it empty, swept, and garnished. Then goeth he, and taketh with himself seven other spirits more wicked than himself, and they enter in and dwell there: and the last state of that man is worse than the first. (Matthew 12:43–45)

> When the chief baker saw that the interpretation was good, he said unto Joseph, "I also was in my dream, and, behold, I had three white baskets on my head: And in the uppermost basket there was of all manner of bakemeats for Pharaoh; and the birds did eat them out of the basket upon my head." And Joseph answered and said, "This is the interpretation thereof: the three baskets are three days: Yet within three days shall Pharaoh lift up thy head from off thee, and shall hang thee on a tree; and birds shall eat thy flesh from off thee." And it came to pass the third day, which was Pharaoh's birthday, that he made a feast unto all his servants: and he lifted up the head of the chief butler and of the chief baker among his servants. And he restored the chief butler unto his butlership again; and he gave the cup into Pharaoh's hand: but he hanged the chief baker: as Joseph had interpreted to them. (Genesis 40:16–22)

This passage shows us how accurate dreams can be; therefore, it is foolishness to assume that the devil does not put evil seeds in and through our dreams. It is our duty as believers to destroy every evil seed the devil has sown in our dreams, for they are a threat to our destiny. If you think you cannot cancel these evil seeds by your faith alone, get some brethren to stand with you in an agreement of prayers.

God can reveal the machinations of the enemy through your dreams, and sometimes even the enemy himself reveals his threats against you in your dreams, so never ignore evil dreams. The chief baker did not do anything about the interpretation that Joseph gave him; the result is that he died just as the dream revealed. A man once told me that every year in the month of June, he has a particular dream, and consequently bad things begin to happen to him. I told him to pray and aggressively reverse every evil decree for his life attached to the month of June. If there is a particular bad dream that keeps occurring in your life, it is time to request for special prayers because your destiny is in danger.

No matter what seed the devil has planted in your life, the power of God will flush it out in the name of Jesus! Take your dreams more seriously. Examine them and ask for interpretation. Not all dreams are bad. Some dreams are from the business of the mind, some are from devil, and some are from God.

> But he answered and said, "Every plant, which my heavenly Father hath not planted, shall be rooted up." (Matthew 15:13)

A nurse once told me that she had breast cancer, and the doctors treating her had lost all hope that she would survive the ordeal. I shared this scripture above and prayed with her. A few months later, she called me and said that the doctors could not find any trace or symptoms of cancer in her, and there is nothing God cannot uproot. Evil seeds are not from God; therefore, they shall be uprooted in the name of Jesus!

Say this prayer: "I release the blood of Jesus in my body. I command every evil seed that was deposited into my body while I was sleeping to die today in the name of Jesus!"

CHAPTER 4

The Diverse Nature of Manipulations

Dreams are important and are a natural phenomenon that is common to virtually every human being. The dream phenomenon is so commonplace that most of us do not take them seriously; neither do we make any effort to analyze or evaluate them in order to find out what they are all about. In fact, some people dismiss any serious attempt at analyzing dreams and regard them as superstitious exercises. Yet dreaming is scriptural. The Bible tells us that God speaks to us through dreams. So can the devil too!

Whether we believe it or not, whether we accept it or not, when we sleep, there are things that happen in our dreams that affect us in the physical.

> The kingdom of heaven is likened unto a man which sowed good seed in his field: But while men slept, his enemy came and sowed tares among the wheat, and went his way. (Matthew 13:24–25)

There is no ambiguity here. When the enemy comes, he does not come to play or sow blessings; he comes to sow bad things into your life. And this is the authoritative Word from Jesus, the Master and Supreme Teacher. He says that there are certain things that witches, demons, and the kingdom of darkness in all its ramifications can do to you in your sleep in order to contaminate your destiny. Jesus is not warning sinners or unbelievers; He is talking to children of the kingdom.

> The field is the life of a man; the good seed is the pre-ordained purpose or vision of God for the man in the kingdom; but the tares are those things that will destroy the vision, such as wicked spirits and contamination in world pleasures. (Matthew 13:38)

The witchcraft spirit, the familiar spirit, the spirit wives and husbands and so on are the children of the devil that come out at night to sow tares among the wheat. Is it any wonder, therefore, that many Christians are being harassed and still suffer all manner of manipulations in their dreams?
Demonic manipulations in dreams occur in various ways:

(1) Forgetting your dreams

One very common form is when someone dreams and when they wake up, he or she cannot recollect any detail of that dream. If you fall into this category all the time, then know that it is time for prayer. What you are experiencing is a typical witchcraft manipulation. This can affect you in two ways:

> (a) If you are unable to recollect or remember your dreams, you cannot know if God is passing a message across to you; neither will you know if the devil is wreaking havoc in your life. How then will you know whether to reject what you saw in your dream or claim it? The desire of the kingdom of darkness is for you to have no recollection of your dreams so that you will not be able to pray or do anything about it. The result is that whatever evil thing has been planted into your life will ultimately become a reality.

(b) The phenomenon of people not recollecting their dreams is a very dangerous one because those who are affected may be operating as blind occult members without knowing it. They are not allowed to know or remember what they do in the occult gatherings. They will participate in all sorts of wicked activities like eating their ritual meat, visiting the river, and so on, without having the slightest clue of what they are doing because their memory has been darkened or covered.

So if you do not remember your dreams, the thing to do is pray that the Holy Spirit will cause you to remember your dreams and that God will enlighten your spiritual understanding.

(2) Not dreaming at all

This is yet another form of manipulation. People who do not dream at all or those who think they do not dream are living a dangerous life just like those mentioned in the earlier example. True, it is not compulsory that one should dream every night or all the time, but not to dream at all is unnatural. Even people born blind have dreams. I have interviewed blind people who confirmed that they do have dreams and very vivid ones too! Now if you do not dream at all, then you need to pray. It may be that the kingdom of darkness has sealed up your spiritual memory.

(3) Using deceptive covers

Another variant of witchcraft manipulations in dreams shows how devious the enemy can be. While demons are attacking you or contaminating your life in your dreams, they assume the faces of people close to you, thereby diverting your attention from the real source of your troubles. Understandably, most people will jump to the conclusion that the faces they see attacking them in their dreams are the architects of their day-to-day woes. Such dreams always lead to hatred toward those faces they see in their dreams. The truth may shock us: Those we have identified as our enemies may be innocent victims of demonic manipulations in dreams. Demonic manipulations in dreams come in numerous forms. Many manifest in diverse forms other than those that have been treated here. However, throughout the course of my counseling, I have come to identify some of these as common examples.

In a lot of cases, these manipulations occur in the lives of Christians. Indeed, there are Christians who are frustrated because the more they pray, the more they are held subject to these evil manipulations. The question which naturally arises is: How is it possible for the kingdom of darkness to gain access or entrance into our lives to manipulate our dreams when the Bible tells us that as children of God, we are surrounded by a wall of fire? There are clear reasons for this.

CHAPTER 5

Why Do Demons Manipulate Our Dreams?

(1) Unbroken covenant

Demons and other forces of darkness are able to distort and twist our dreams as a result of some unbroken covenants in our lives. This is why as a born-again Christian, it is possible that the more you bind and cast out these demons, the more they visit you in your sleep to torment you.

We are often tied to these covenants through mistakes made by our parents in their desperate search for children or by our observance of what we regard as *simple* traditional ceremonies and rites. We may also open the gateway by our own unwholesome religious or spiritual practices. And sometimes, these covenants and initiations are renewed by what we eat or drink in our dreams.

In all of these, one thing is obviously true: Somewhere along the line, the Word of God has been breached. When we go to offer sacrifices to idols we have created for ourselves (by ourselves), we offend God and attract to ourselves very grave consequences. The Bible in *2 Kings* reminds us of how such an act of deviation incensed God:

> But he walked in the way of the kings of Israel, yea, and made his son to pass through the fire, according to the abominations of the heathen, whom the LORD cast out from before the

children of Israel. And he sacrificed and burnt incense in the high places, and on the hills, and under every green tree. (2 Kings 16:3–4)

And they left all the commandments of the LORD their God, and made them molten images, even two calves, and made a grove, and worshipped all the host of heaven and served Baal. And they caused their sons and daughters to pass through the fire, and used divination and enchantments, and sold themselves to do evil in the sight of the LORD, to provoke him to anger. (2 Kings 17:16–17)

And he made his son pass through the fire, and observed the times, and used enchantments, and dealt with familiar spirits and wizards: he wrought much wickedness in the sight of the LORD, to provoke him to anger. (2 Kings 21:6)

(2) Parental, prenatal, and antenatal activities

Right from birth, most of us have been marked down and dedicated to particular idols in our families, villages, and places where we live or have lived. For some of us, this was done even before we were born. This is just one of the primary ways by which the enemy gains access into our lives.

In their search for children, some parents have dined with the devil. Out of sheer desperation, many parents have led their unborn babies into trouble. Some people want a child at any cost and would go to any length to obtain one. Some are perhaps blessed with a number of girls and would do anything to have the elusive yet desirable baby boy or vice versa.

In their search, such parents visit shrines and sacred rivers and consult with water and familiar spirits, indeed all types of evil spirits.

They are made to drink all manner of concoctions, buy all kinds of ritual items, and participate in all kinds of rituals.

For others, the problem is that their babies are delivered stillborn. In order to prevent a reoccurrence, ritual items are demanded by the fetish priests to appease their gods. In addition, when such babies are born alive, they are inflicted with marks and incisions and sometimes have to wear amulets around their legs for "protection."

All these marks, incisions, and ritual objects automatically link these babies to demonic covenants.

(3) Traditional naming ceremony

The traditional naming ceremony takes different forms in different areas of Nigeria and Africa, but one thing that is common to them all is the offering of ritual items like sugarcane, sugar, honey, alligator pepper, dried fish, kola nut, a local clay pot, dried rat and dried lizard, among other things. The question people fail to ask is, "What do these items have to do with naming a child?"

In reality, these items are offered as sacrifice to the evil spirit or the familiar spirit controlling a family, and every family has one! You may not know this. Naively, people assume that they are just performing some harmless and arcane traditional rites.

Now for any new child to belong to the community, a sacrifice of ritual objects has to be made. After you have paid the price, the witchcraft spirit or any other spirit active in that family enters the child. From that moment on, a relationship has been established. Having paid in full of what may be considered as your "*membership fees*," it is now easy for the evil forces to attack you, should the need arise. All they have to do is go to the shrine at which you were dedicated and communicate with the resident idol. And because you have fully paid up your dues, your spirit, soul, and body will respond whenever they wish to make contact. You are now linked to their network, and they will keep monitoring your life

(4) Traditional marriage ceremony

Just as the case with the traditional child naming ceremony, the traditional marriage ceremony requires participants to present similar ritual items like the ones earlier mentioned—including alcoholic drinks.

There are Christians who object to this ceremony, but in most cases, they are not firm with their objection. Sooner or later they succumb to the pressure and accept compromises that attract the same divine disapproval and punishment as they would have received if they had gone through the actual rites.

The compromise may take the form of the bride and groom paying for or providing the required ritual items without presenting themselves to receive any incantations or prayers offered to idols.

However, have you ever stopped to ask, *"What happens to these items? Where are they taken? What is their final destination? To what gods are they being offered?"*

The truth is that portions of these items are taken to the villages and offered in sacrifice to ancestral and family idols, thereby establishing and reinforcing covenants with them. In cases where they are not taken to the village, some overzealous relations would end up invoking the "spirit of the ancestors" and some other family gods. In either case, demonic spirits are released to follow and monitor the couple wherever they go.

Always make a habit of asking questions and seeking answers. Seek and you will find!

(5) Demonic religious/spiritual literature

Not long after I became a Christian, I found myself reading a dangerous book in search of knowledge, *The Sixth and Seventh Book of Moses.* Luckily, God ministered to me to stop reading the book and to burn it so that I would not open the gate for evil spirits to come into my life. There are Christians who are still reading and experimenting with such books. Moses (in the Bible) never wrote any sixth or seventh book.

For those with a Nigerian or African background, membership of and participation in the religious activities of the "white garment" or syncretic churches (they are called white garment churches because members are required to be uniformly dressed in flowing white soutanes) exposes you to all kinds of demonic spirits—especially water or marine spirits.

As those who have passed through these churches will confirm, people seeking solutions to spiritual problems are often subjected to unscriptural baths in streams, rivers, and at road junctions, with all manners of strange invocations. This is ultimately a gateway for demons, if ever there was one!

CHAPTER 6

Some Common Dream Patterns

Let me state for the record that I do not interpret dreams. It is only God Who has the divine key for interpreting dreams. I would like to advise those who write books claiming to interpret dreams to be careful of their interpretations. In just about every case, the same dream doesn't usually have the same meaning in the Bible. Signs and symbols in a dream can be very relative and personal.

Having said this, I should point out that whatever explanations I give here regarding dreams have been informed by my personal experience and confirmation through the process of counseling. In the course of counseling people over the years, I have heard them relate certain kinds of dreams over and over again, and the manifestations in their physical lives have been remarkably similar.

For example, there are people whose dreams always come true. Others have dreams which present one picture, only for the opposite to manifest in the physical. What do these patterns indicate?

Dreams that always come true

If you are a believer and your dreams often come to pass, then God may be showing you things that are about to happen. The reason God reveals such things is so that you can pray about them. It is not only believers who have dreams that come to pass. There are unbelievers who have similar experiences. The question is whether such dreams come from the spirit of God.

Dreams that manifest the opposite

If your dreams always turn out to be the opposite of what you dreamt about, then there is the need to pray that God should show what exactly is going on. The fact that you are seeing negative things in your dreams does not automatically mean that terrible things are about to happen in the physical. Sometimes when you dream and God presents you with a negative picture, you end up having something positive manifest.

For example, Joseph dreamt that his elders would bow to him, the youngest. In the part of the world where I come from, it is unheard of and an abomination, for an elder to bow to a younger person. For someone with my background and origin, such a dream would be regarded as a bad dream and would certainly not be seen as a sign or move of God.

A key point to note, however, is that the regularity of a particular kind of dream, irrespective of whether a dream is good or bad, indicates that either God or the kingdom of darkness is passing a message on to us. This is the case as long as it is a regular dream.

I should also point out that it is not every dream that is of the devil. This is why we need divine guidance to interpret our dreams. Sometimes, our dreams are a product of our inflamed imagination.

If you are sufficiently burdened by a matter before falling asleep, do not be surprised to find yourself having lurid dreams about the same matter in your sleep.

There are some demonic dreams of which we shall provide some insights in the light of the Bible and practical experience in the field of deliverance.

Having babies, getting married, or being pregnant in dreams

If you regularly have dreams in which you find yourself getting pregnant, married, or carrying babies, chances are that you are already married to a spirit wife or husband in the spirit realm. Again, this can be traced to the covenants made by some of our parents in their desperate search for children.

Now because you are already married to these demons in the spirit realm, they will make sure that your family life (if you are married in the physical) is hell. You will find yourself staggering from one matrimonial crisis to another.

If you are not yet married, these forces will chase away any man or woman showing interest in you. The reason is simple: The moment you get married in the physical, you will devote yourself to your real living wife or husband, and the spirit spouse does not like that.

It may well be that you are in search of a child, but you regularly have dreams where a strange man makes love to you. The result would be that while in the spirit realm, you give birth to babies, and in the physical, you have miscarriages, stillbirths, and babies who die shortly after birth. As you are well aware, both men and women have God-given reproductive eggs. When these demons have sex with you in your dreams, they contaminate these physical eggs; thereby ensuring that by the time they are released, they are already dead.

Sometimes, an expectant mother may constantly see blood in her dreams. This should be an indication to her that her inability to carry her pregnancy to full term and have a successful delivery is not only just a medical problem but also one that needs to be handled spiritually also.

Eating and drinking in dreams

Again, it is not every time you eat or drink in your dreams that it signifies something evil. It is probably demonic if it becomes a regular and/or reoccurring phenomenon. The consequences or implications of eating in a dream vary, but two examples you are about to read should illustrate the dangers.

A Christian sister once told me a story of how she found herself in a dream with her close friend (who was also a Christian) eating a local Nigerian delicacy—roasted plantain (popularly called *boli*).

Suddenly, one of them realized that they did not sanctify the food before they started eating it. Despite the fact that they had worked their way through half of the meal, they still prayed and blessed it.

As soon as they finished praying and opened their eyes (the sister was still dreaming), the leftover food in their hands was transformed into the mutilated remains of a baby's hand, still dripping with fresh blood!

Clearly, this shows that some of the foods we eat in our dreams are not what they appear to be on the surface. These foods may be offered to initiate us into covenants or cults. It is possible to that the meat in this dream is their share from the occult rituals of an occult group.

If these Christians sisters now find themselves initiated into this cult—flying or attending meetings in their dreams with strange people—they would be shocked and surprised. Through their carelessness, they allowed the devil to gain entry in their lives in the dream.

Sometimes, diseases are deposited into our lives through the things we eat in our dreams. A few years back, I was called to pray for a lady living in a town in Nigeria, who was ill. When I used to know this lady, there was nothing wrong with her hands, legs, or any part of her body. By the time I got to her after receiving the call, her hands and legs were grotesquely twisted and curled.

I asked what had happened, and she told me that in her sleep (dream), she ate something and woke up to find her hands and legs shaking. Later both hands and legs got swollen and slowly became twisted. As I began to pray for her, the Lord revealed to me what had happened to her. There are many other cases like hers. People eat in their dreams and find cancer tumors or other deadly diseases in their bodies.

Eating in the dream could also lead to the weakening of one's spiritual life. People have reported the loss of the urge to pray or study the Bible after eating in their dreams.

Flying in the dream

If you fly around in your dreams, chances are that you are engaged in occult practices or have partaken in the rituals performed for the protection of family members, such as witchcraft, Halloween, etc.

Some other people, who have experienced this phenomenon, also fly when there is a threat to their lives in their dreams. For instance, someone may be about to kill them, and they suddenly take flight.

Some Christians who still fly in their dreams think that it is the Holy Spirit propelling them! This is not so. Flying around with your arms and legs spread wide and your tie dangling downward is certainly not the manner children of God are expected to travel to heaven. If the Holy Spirit is at work, we must be lifted up the same way Jesus Christ was lifted.

Traveling in the dream

From experience while counseling, I have observed that people who keep having dreams about traveling or trekking but never arriving at a destination are often locked in day-to-day struggles (in life) with little or nothing to show for their efforts.

Being pressed down physically

This is an experience many people have had. You just have this feeling of being pressed down by some weighty, formless, and invisible object. You want to push out from under the weight, but you can't. You feel like shouting, but cannot get your tongue to form the words.

This is a typical witchcraft operation, with the forces of darkness attempting to deposit some evil things in you. If you have been subjected to this terrifying experience, then you need to present yourself for a deliverance checkup because the mark of these forces of darkness is already upon you.

Being chased by wild men, animals, etc.

This often suggests that some form of attack is underway, and one has to be prayerful to ward it off.

Associating with the dead in dreams

It is certainly not a good development when you regularly find yourself associating, chatting, and eating with dead people in your dreams. In some cases, it could lead to death. It is generally indicative of the spirit of necromancy at work.

Associating with old acquaintances, schoolmates, etc.

Again, regularity is the key. If you keep finding yourself in the company of associates whom you have left behind for years, or you keep seeing yourself in (the poor setting) your village, hometown, or old neighborhood, which you have not visited for years, then there is a battle on the way. You have to pray against setbacks, retrogression, and demonic associations.

Marks and incisions

People sometimes wake up in the morning to discover strange marks and incisions on their bodies. This indicates some form of initiation or the renewal of some former initiation. Invariably, proper investigation will show that there is something demonic in the victims' origin or past.

The cases touched upon here are by no means exhaustive. And again, I repeat that it is only God Who has the divine keys for interpreting dreams.

This exercise enables us to see that what happens to us in our dreams should not be trifled with. We are spirit beings: Our lives in the physical are often determined by events that have taken place in the spirit realm. That is why we have to be alert and scrutinize our dreams when they occur.

CHAPTER 7

Warfare Prayers against Dream Manipulations

Heavenly Father, I present myself to You today—spirit, soul, and body; for cleansing through the blood of Jesus, from all curses in my family. I renounce all known and unknown curses as well as unholy covenants in *Jesus's name*. I apply the blood of Jesus to my whole system for purification from all curses. Christ has redeemed me from the curse of the law. Therefore, I am free in *Jesus's name*. Amen.

(i) Prayer of preparation before deliverance

I confess with my lips that JESUS is Lord and in my heart I believe that You raised Him from the dead. (*Romans 10:9*)

I repent of my past sins and I admit and confess that I have sinned (mention the sin) and I believe that You are faithful and just to cleanse me from all unrighteousness. (*Luke 13:3*)

> I call upon You, Lord JESUS, to cleanse me from all sin and unrighteousness by Your blood. (*1 John 1:7*)
>
> Everyone who calls upon the name of the Lord shall be saved. (*Romans 10:13*)
>
> Christ purchased our freedom (redeeming us) from the curse (doom) of the Law (and its condemnation) by becoming a curse for us. (*Galatians 3:13*)
>
> For it is written (in the Scriptures), "Cursed is everyone who hangs on a tree (crucified)" (*Deuteronomy 21:23*)

I confess, repent, and ask for forgiveness of all sins listed in *Deuteronomy 27 and 28*, and I break the curses associated with those sins.

(ii) Scriptures for deliverance and spiritual warfare

The Word of God is the greatest weapon of deliverance. There are certain scriptures that can be used as a weapon for your deliverance. You must keep on confessing these scriptures so that you can obtain and retain your deliverance.

Any bondage that emanates from the kingdom of darkness can be nullified through the Word of God. The Word of God will open your eyes to whatever it takes to obtain your deliverance.

Confessing the scriptures below will arm you with the weapons needed for obtaining victory in spiritual battles. These scriptures will also open the gates of deliverance to those held captive through curses, covenants, and satanic bondage. You need to read these scriptures over and over again until you are completely set free. These verses will also grant you spiritual immunity.

> And I will feed them that oppress thee with their own flesh; and they shall be drunken with their own blood, as with sweet wine: and all flesh shall know that I the LORD am thy Savior and the Redeemer, the mighty One of Jacob. (Isaiah 49:26)

> And I will deliver thee out of the hand of the wicked, and I will redeem thee out of the hand of the terrible. (Jeremiah 15:21)

> The Spirit of the Lord is upon me, because he hath anointed me to preach the gospel to the poor; he hath sent me to heal the brokenhearted, to preach deliverance to the captives, and recovering of sight to the blind, to set at liberty them that are bruised, To preach the acceptable year of the Lord. (Luke 4:18–19)

> For the LORD thy God walketh in the midst of thy camp, to deliver thee, and to give up thine enemies before thee; therefore shall thy camp be holy: that he see no unclean thing in thee, and turn away from thee. (Deuteronomy 23:14)

> Let the redeemed of the LORD say so, whom he hath redeemed from the hand of the enemy; And gathered them out of the lands, from the east, and from the west, from the north, and from the south. They wandered in the wilderness in a solitary way; they found no city to dwell in. Hungry and thirsty, their soul fainted in them. (Psalm 107:2–5)

And from the days of John the Baptist until now the kingdom of heaven suffereth violence, and the violent take it by force. (Matthew 11:12)

No weapon that is formed against thee shall prosper; and every tongue that shall rise against thee in judgment thou shall condemn. This is the heritage of the servants of the LORD, and their righteousness is of me, saith the LORD. (Isaiah 54:17)

But the LORD your God ye shall fear; and he shall deliver you out of the hand of all your enemies. (2 Kings 17:39)

When I cry unto thee, then shall mine enemies turn back: this I know; for God is for me. (Psalm 56:9)

Shall the prey be taken from the mighty, or the lawful captive delivered? But thus saith the LORD, Even the captives of the mighty shall be taken away, and the prey of the terrible shall be delivered: for I will contend with him that contendeth with thee, and I will save thy children. (Isaiah 49:24–25)

And I will make thee unto this people a fenced brazen wall: and they shall fight against thee, but they shall not prevail against thee: for I am with thee to save thee and to deliver thee, saith the LORD. (Jeremiah 15:20)

For thou hast broken the yoke of his burden, and the staff of his shoulder, the rod of his oppressor, as in the day of Midian. For every battle of the warrior is with confused noise, and garments rolled in blood; but this shall be with burning and fuel of fire. (Isaiah 9:4–5)

And there was delivered unto him the book of the prophet Esaias. And when he had opened the book, he found the place where it was written, The Spirit of the Lord is upon me, because he hath anointed me to preach the gospel to the poor; he hath sent me to heal the brokenhearted, to preach deliverance to the captives, and recovering of sight to the blind, to set at liberty them that are bruised. (Luke 4:17–18)

Thou art my hiding place; thou shalt preserve me from trouble; thou shalt compass me about with songs of deliverance. Selah. (Psalm 32:7)

(iii) Repentance and confession

Thank You, Lord, for dying for my sins, for Your glorious resurrection, and for making me a new creature in CHRIST JESUS by faith in Your precious.

According to *Romans 10:9*, I confess with my lips that JESUS is Lord and in my heart I believe that you raised him from the dead.

According to *Luke 13:3*, I repent of my past sins, and I admit and confess that I have sinned, and I believe that You are faithful and just to cleanse me from all unrighteousness.

I call upon You, Lord JESUS, to cleanse me from all sin and unrighteousness by Your blood *(1 John 1:7)*.

As your Word says in *Romans 10:13*, "Everyone who calls upon the name of the Lord will be saved."

1. "I am the BODY OF CHRIST. I overcome evil with good" *(1 Corinthians 12:27; Romans 12:21)*.

2. "I am of God. I have overcome the world. He who is in me is greater than he who is in the world" *(1 John 4:4).*
3. "I am established in righteousness. I am far from terror and oppression. I shall not fear. I walk through the valley of the shadow of death. I will fear no evil. CHRIST is with me. His rod and His staff comfort me" *(Isaiah 54:14; Psalm 23:4).*
4. "My righteousness is from THE LORD. No weapon formed against me shall prosper. I condemn tongues that rise against me. This is my heritage as a servant of THE LORD" *(Isaiah 54:17).*
5. "No evil shall befall me. No plague shall come near me or my dwelling. He gives His angels charge over me. They keep me in my ways" *(Psalm 91:10–11).*
6. "I delight in the LAW OF THE LORD; I meditate in it day and night. I am like a tree planted by the rivers of water bringing forth abundant fruit in season. My leaves do not wither. Whatever I do prospers" *(Psalm 1:2–3).*
7. "JESUS CHRIST gave Himself for my sins. I have been delivered from this world according to the WILL OF GOD" *(Galatians 1:4).*
8. "I have been given authority over the power of the enemy to trample on serpents and scorpions. Nothing shall by any means hurt me. I possess the keys of the KINGDOM OF HEAVEN. Whatever I bind on earth is bound in Heaven. Whatever I loose on earth is loosed in Heaven. I bind principalities, powers, rulers of darkness, and hosts of wickedness that oppose me, my family, and the work of God. I lose THE HOLY GHOST, mighty warring angels, and the BLOOD OF JESUS CHRIST to cover, protect, bless, and minister to me, my family, and those doing THE WORK OF GOD" *(Luke 10:19; Matthew 16:19; Ephesians 6:12).*
9. "I take the shield of faith. I quench the fiery darts of the wicked one. I overcome by THE BLOOD OF THE LAMB and word of my testimony. I love not my life unto death. My life belongs to CHRIST JESUS" *(Ephesians 6:16; Revelations 12:11).*

10. "I submit to GOD, resist the devil and he flees from me. I draw near to GOD. He draws near to me baptizing me with the Holy Ghost and fire" *(James 4:7–8; Matthew 3:11)*.
11. "I am in the way of righteousness. I find life. There is no death in or around me. CHRIST redeemed me from the curse of the law. He became a curse for me. I walk in the blessings of THE HOLY SPIRIT. I am truly blessed" *(Proverbs 12:28)*.
12. "THE SPIRIT that raised JESUS CHRIST from the dead dwells in me. He gives life to my mortal body. No sickness or infirmity has any place in me. CHRIST was bruised for my iniquities, the chastisement of my peace was upon Him, and by His stripes I am healed" *(Romans 8:11; Isaiah 53:5)*.
13. "I am the temple of the LIVING GOD. I do not let THE WORD OF GOD depart from my eyes. I keep it in the midst of my heart. It is life to me and health to my flesh" *(Proverbs 4:21–22)*.
14. "CHRIST came so that I can have life and have it more abundantly. I delight myself in THE LORD. He gives me the desires of my heart" *(John 10:10; Psalm. 37:4)*.
15. "My GOD is supplying my needs according to His riches in glory by CHRIST JESUS. He is my shepherd. I shall not want" *(Philippians 4:19; Psalm 23:1)*.

(iv) Breaking evil covenants and curses from the bloodline!

> Then I will set my face against that man, and against his family, and will cut him off, and all that go a whoring after him, to commit whoredom with Molech, from among their people. And the soul that turneth after such as have familiar spirits, and after wizards, to go a whoring after them, I will even set my face against that soul, and will cut him off from among his people. (Leviticus 20:5–6)

This is not automatic, it must be applied like salvation, healing, Holy Ghost baptism, and so on. If you don't confess God's Word with your mouth and believe in your heart, nothing will happen.

Now it is time to break the curses of our bloodline. When these curses are broken, I have found out that the demon is ready to get out because he doesn't have a place to stay anymore.

First of all, begin to worship the Lord. You are His tabernacle. You are a dwelling place for the Lord. God Almighty dwells in you. You are His vessel.

Prayer points:

1. I break the curses of idle words and abominations that caused generations before me to go after the gods of this world in the name of Jesus!
2. I break the curse of idolatry and paganistic practices and command them to lose their hold on my life in the name of Jesus!
3. I break the curses of "the wanderer and the vagabond." I break every curse of rebellion, disobedience, and not obeying the Word of God. I command selfishness and greed to lose their hold on me in the name of Jesus!
4. I break the curse of the city where I was born and everything that has affected me from that city in the name of Jesus!
5. I break every curse on my fields, lands, and inheritance. I break every curse on the fruit of my body, on my children, and on my generation in the name of Jesus!
6. I break every curse concerning the work of my hands, the increase of my wealth, and the blessings of my land in the name of Jesus!
7. I break all curses on my going out and my coming in, on my sitting down and my rising up in the name of Jesus!
8. I break the curse on my basket and my storehouse in the name of Jesus!

9. I break every curse set up by Satan, to bring defeat into my generation in the name of Jesus!
10. I command all lawlessness and rebellion to cease in the name of Jesus!
11. I break the curse of confusion. I command the spirit of confusion, the spirit of Babylon—the harlot system, the whorish nature of the flirtatious woman that goes whoring after other gods, to lose its hold on my life right now in the name of Jesus!
12. I come against the curse of Babylon. I go back four generations and break its hold on my life in the name of Jesus!
13. I come against all rebuke, blasphemy, and every curse of damnation that has been spoken my bloodline for the past four generations in the name of Jesus!
14. I break everything that took away my self-worth in the name of Jesus!
15. I come against the spirit of destruction. I command this curse of destruction to be loosed from my generation in the mighty name of Jesus!
16. I command the curse of all forms of evil: backbiting, slander, contention, anger, hatred, and so on to come out in the name of Jesus!
17. I come against every pestilence. I break the curse of poverty and command it to lose its hold on my life in the name of Jesus!
18. I break the curses of stealing, deceit, incest, illegitimacy, and sodomy. I come against the spirits of pride and self-righteousness. I command all religious spirits to lose their hold on my life. Everything that has been stolen from me, I command an immediate restoration in the name of Jesus!
19. I break the curses of consumption and fever, inflammation, fiery heat, sword and drought, blasting and mildew, which continue to pursue me. I come against all diseases and infirmities in the name of Jesus!
20. I break the curse of brass—not hearing, no sight, no vision in the name of Jesus!

21. I command condemnation to lose its hold on my life in the name of Jesus!
22. I break the curse of powdered soil and dust from the heavens in the name of Jesus!
23. I break the curse that causes me to be struck down by my enemies. I command the spirits of failure and lack of vision to lose its hold on my life in the name of Jesus!
24. I break the curse of premature death and the curse of boils, blood diseases, and tumors in the name of Jesus!
25. I lose the curse of cancer from my body in the name of Jesus!
26. I command bitterness (the roots of bitterness), resentment, and unforgiveness to lose its hold on my life. I break the curse of molestation and frigidity in the name of Jesus!
27. I break everything that would make me the tail (i.e., beneath always) in the name of Jesus!
28. I come against depression, insanity, and retardation in the name of Jesus!
29. Under the covering of the blood of Jesus, I break the curse of scurvy, itching, all skin diseases, herpes, psoriasis, and all infirmities or conditions that don't heal. I come against the torment of itching and nervousness in the name of Jesus!
30. I break the curse of shingles, madness, and insanity in the name of Jesus!
31. I break the curse of blindness and no spiritual insight in the name of Jesus!
32. I come against the spirit of dismay, despair, mental anguish, and mental depression in the name of Jesus!
33. By the power in the blood of Jesus, I cancel everything that has bruised my life as a result of generational curses in the name of Jesus!
34. I call on heaven and earth to witness that I will no longer be bound by poverty. I come against the enemy coming in and robbing me of all things that are precious and good in the name of Jesus!

35. I break the curse of lust, promiscuity, adultery, fornication, bestiality, and perversion. I cancel your assignments in my life in the name of Jesus!
36. I break the curse of sore boils in the knees and legs, causing a lack of balance. I decree healing from the crown of my head to the soles of my feet in the name of Jesus!
37. I break the curse of all the diseases of Egypt and all types of diseases which could run in my bloodline: arthritis, diabetes, hypertension, heart trouble, nervousness, and all other blood-related diseases, weakness in the knees, rheumatism, neck and backaches, and pain in the spinal cord in the name of Jesus!
38. I break the curse of edema and swelling. I command heart attack and stroke to be broken off from my bloodline in the name of Jesus!
39. I break the curse that would allow the enemy to pursue and overtake me in the name of Jesus!
40. I break all curses of mind control and witchcraft in my bloodline, and I command every demon to lose its hold over my life in the name of Jesus!
41. I break every curse pronounced into my life by false prophets, and I command that all false teachings and errors that I have heard and accepted be cancelled and removed from my life in the name of Jesus!
42. I break the curse of unbelievers in my household: from the lives of my father, mother, siblings, children, husband, or wife in the name of Jesus!
43. I break the curse of laziness, and I command the spirit of passivity to lose its hold on my life in the name of Jesus!
44. I command the witch, the warlock, and the generation that has been filtered with these evils to depart in the name of Jesus!
45. I break the curse of the spirit of Jezebel, and I lose that theatrical spirit that always wants to be seen and heard in the name of Jesus!

46. I break the curse of verbal and physical abuse (many times as children, we were whipped or beaten and verbally abused, and this has left a mark on our personality). I come against the spirit of abuse, and I break the curses of damnation in the name of Jesus!
47. O Lord, baptize me with the fire of deliverance in the name of Jesus!
48. I bind all demonic spirits attached to covenants and curses and command you to come out of my life in the name of Jesus!
49. Father, let the blood of Jesus erase all my sins that opened the doors to the curses recorded in the Bible in the name of Jesus!
50. By the power of resurrection, I reverse every negative decree already signed against me, and that can affect me in any form in the name of Jesus!
51. Father, reverse every negative order placed over my destiny in the name of Jesus!
52. Holy Spirit, wherever my name has been written or is mentioned, let Your voice respond on my behalf in the name of Jesus!
53. Holy Spirit, confuse my enemies in their own camp in the name of Jesus!
54. Let the power of God tear down everything the devil has put together concerning my name in the name of Jesus!
55. Under the new covenant, which is the covenant of the blood of Jesus, I renounce all the evil works I have done in the lives of innocent people through my membership with these demonic associations, and I ask the Almighty God to forgive me and cleanse me with the blood of Jesus in the name of Jesus!
56. I request the blood of Jesus to flush out my system, purify my body, and cleanse me from all evil things I have eaten in any of the demonic cults or associations in the name of Jesus!

57. Wherever my name has been initiated either consciously or unconsciously, I withdraw and cancel my name from their registers with the blood of Jesus in the name of Jesus!

(v) Prayers against the manipulation of witchcraft and familiar spirits

> Thou shalt not suffer a witch to live. (Exodus 22:18)

> Regard not them that have familiar spirits, neither seek after wizards, to be defiled by them: I am the LORD your God. (Leviticus 19:31)

Witchcraft is commonly defined as the use of magical powers to influence, control, or manipulate people or events. It is commonly known as sorcery and has been an integral part of the folklore of many societies for centuries.

Prayer points:

1. I deactivate the power of every satanic food that I have eaten in my dream in the name of Jesus!
2. Every arrow of darkness militating against my destiny, I return back to sender in the name of Jesus!
3. I reverse all evil pronouncements aimed at me into blessings in the name of Jesus!
4. By the power in the blood of Jesus, I break all witchcraft curses working against my ministry in the name of Jesus!
5. By the power in the blood of Jesus, I break all witchcraft curses working against my family in the name of Jesus!
6. By the power in the blood of Jesus, I break every conscious or unconscious initiation into witchcraft by my grandparents, parents, or by myself in the name of Jesus!

7. By the power in the blood of Jesus, I paralyze all witchcraft curses from my foundation that are working against my job/career/business in the name of Jesus!
8. I break the power of every "placental manipulation" of my destiny by any familiar spirits in the name of Jesus!
9. Arrows of the Almighty God! Arise and persecute my persecutors, pursue my pursuers, attack my attackers and torment my tormentors in the name of Jesus!
10. Finger of God! Arise; destroy my destroyers and arrest my arrestor in the name of Jesus!
11. By the power in the blood of Jesus, I recover all that I have lost to the powers of the night either physically or through immorality in my dreams in the name of Jesus!
12. I break every link to witchcraft in my life in the name of Jesus!
13. I break every power of witchcraft from my mother's and/or father's family that has been affecting my life in the name of Jesus!
14. Holy Ghost, destroy all the central control towers of witchcraft activities over my destiny in the name of Jesus!
15. Satan, I take authority over your kingdom and over all your programs against my life in the name of Jesus!
16. I disown every familiar spirit in the name of Jesus!
17. I refuse to be under any familiar spirit that is presently ruling over my family in the name of Jesus!
18. By the power in the blood of Jesus, I break every evil covenant or dedication to the place of my birth in the name of Jesus!
19. I break the power of limitation through every familiar spirit working against my destiny in the name of Jesus!
20. By the power in the blood of Jesus and by the power of the Holy Ghost, my family, and I will make heaven in the name of Jesus!

(vi) Deliverance from spirit husband or wife

> Blotting out the handwriting of ordinances that was against us, which was contrary to us, and took it out of the way, nailing it to his cross. (Colossians 2:14)

A "spirit spouse" is a specific person with a particular face who relates with you consistently as a husband or a wife. In most cases, the spirit husband or wife may appear with someone else's face. The relationship of a "spirit spouse" is not limited to dreams alone. A lady once told me that whenever she is preparing to get married, a well-dressed man will appear to her in her dream, warning her not to ever get married, and that if she did, her husband (in the physical) will die. (The rest of this story and other stories can be found in this book.)

Prayer points

1. I renounce every marital vows or agreements entered into by my ancestors or my immediate parents on my behalf now or before my birth in the name of Jesus!
2. I break and deactivate all vows or covenants entered into with a spirit husband or wife in the name of Jesus!
3. By faith, I withdraw every engagement material, visible or invisible, presented to the spirit world on my behalf in the name of Jesus!
4. I command the fire of God to burn to ashes the spiritual wedding gown (or tuxedo), rings, photographs, marriage certificate, and all other materials used for the wedding in the name of Jesus!
5. I break every demonic blood covenant as a result of having sex, food, or ceremonies in my dream with a spirit husband or wife in the name of Jesus!
6. Let all demonic children who I have had (consciously or unconsciously) in the spirit realm be consumed by fire in the name of Jesus!

7. By the power in the blood of Jesus and under the new covenant, I withdraw my sperm, my blood, my destiny, and any other part of my body deposited on the altar of a spirit husband or wife in the name of Jesus!
8. I receive spiritual authority to break all marital vows and covenants and to affect an everlasting divorce between the spirit husband or wife and myself in the name of the Father, the Son, and the Holy Ghost!
9. I call on heaven and earth to witness this day that I return all demonic properties in my possession back to the spirit world, including symbols, dowry, kola, and whatsoever was presented on the satanic altar or shrine for the marriage ceremony in the name of Jesus!
10. Let the blood of Jesus purge my system of all wrongful sex and all demonic deposits in the name of Jesus!
11. Let the floodlight of the Holy Ghost search my body and expose and destroy every demonic mark, tag, or embargo deposited in my life in the name of Jesus!
12. I command every strange image, object, or symbol deposited by the spirit husband or wife to come out of my life in the name of Jesus!
13. I send my body to the heavenly surgical room for a complete operation to repair, restore, or put right any damage done to any part of my body and/or my earthly marriage by the spirit husband or wife in the name of Jesus!
14. I reject and renounce the demonic name given to me by the spirit husband or wife, and I soak myself in the blood of Jesus and cancel every demonic mark attached to such names in the name of Jesus!
15. I request the Judge of heaven and earth to issue a standing decree order of restriction to every spirit husband or wife, harassing me in my dreams in the mighty name of Jesus!
16. I destroy every demonic power assigned to destabilize my earthly marriage and ability to bear children in the name of Jesus!

17. May the Lord rebuke every demonic agent commissioned from the spirit husband or wife to cause misunderstanding between my spouse and I in the name of Jesus!
18. By the blood of Jesus, I renounce every marital creed and stipulation done in the spirit world that is affecting my earthly marital vows and stipulations in the name of Jesus!
19. With immediate effect, I abandon and disown any spiritual children attached to my name from the spirit husband or wife in the name of Jesus!

(vii) Prayers against dream manipulations

Let me say this: As mentioned in my book, if you don't dream, you are in trouble; this is because dream(s) is one of the ways God speaks and reveals things to His Children in these last days *(See Job 33:18; Acts 2:16–18).*

Bad dreams are pointers to something bad happening to you now or that something evil is going to happen to you. Bad dreams are real, so the Bible is full with prayer against bad dreams that can help you cancel out the effect of those dreams.

So if you are looking for prayer against bad dreams of any kind, this prayer points will help.

Prayer points

1. Lord, I thank You for the grace and the ability You have given to me to dream and receive visions. Lord, I thank You for this precious gift.
2. Father, Your Word says that when I lie down, I shall not be afraid and my sleep shall be sweet (Proverbs 3:24).
3. Therefore, I cancel every satanic manipulation in my dreams in the name of Jesus.
4. I pray that every day of my life, my sleep shall be sweet and blessed in Jesus's name.

5. I receive the grace and ability to sleep and wake up without nightmares in Jesus's name. I rebuke every spirit of sleeplessness in the mighty name of Jesus Christ.
6. I reject and rebuke every spirit of darkness sent to attack me during my sleep in Jesus's name.
7. Any evil dream spirit assigned to my ancestral lineage and which has also been dispatched to me and my lineage, by the fire and power of the Holy Spirit, be rendered powerless and turned back from me now from in Jesus's mighty name.
8. I bind evil witchcraft manipulation movements that manipulate and influence my dreams negatively in the mighty name of Jesus.
9. Father, in the mighty name of Jesus, I cast out every demonic manipulation and evil spirit agent sent on assignment to frustrate or destroy my life through evil dreams and evil actions. I thereby disconnect my spirit, soul, and body from wicked spiritual powers that projects evil dreams and covenants into my life in Jesus's name
10. I reverse all the attacks that the Satan has had on my sleep in Jesus's name. I pray and decree that all the plans that the enemy has on my sleep be destroyed. Amen.
11. I sanctify everywhere and every place I lie down to sleep with the blood of Jesus Christ. I sanctify every material I lie down to sleep upon with the blood of Jesus Christ.
12. All generational, curses, and family inherited curse from my bloodline and evil influences of my maternal and paternal lineage, which linked me to demonic manipulations through evil dreams, I command now, be destroy now out of my life in Jesus's name.
13. I command Holy Ghost fire to burn every ancestral or generational material or connection to evil dreams in my life now in Jesus's name.
14. By the power of the Holy Spirit, I break every covenant and agreement of evil that tied me to evil dream in the name of Jesus.

15. I overcome family inherited curses, ancestral powers, demonic agreements from my bloodline manipulating my dream life by the blood of Jesus Christ.
16. I cover my soul, my spirit, and my body with the blood of Jesus Christ. I forbid every negative and demonic influence over my mind. I declare that my mind will constantly reject demonic nightmares in Jesus's name.
17. In the name of Jesus Christ, I deny every demonic access to my dream life and any evil spirit assigned to work against my mind and prepare it for evil dream.
18. I free my mind from evil thoughts, imagination, and words sent to attack my mind in preparation for evil dreams in Jesus's name.
19. I pull down every stronghold created in my mind for evil dreams in Jesus's name. I cover my mind with the blood of Jesus Christ.
20. In the name of Jesus Christ, I disconnect myself from any known and unknown human satanic agents that are influencing evil dreams in my life.
21. In the name of Jesus, I take authority over every cell in my body, every organ and the entire system of my body, I forbid and reject any demonic spirit from having dominion over them in Jesus's name.
22. By the power of the Holy Spirit, I receive divine healing and restoration of any cell, organ, or system of my body, which the devil has affected in dream.
23. By the power of the Holy Spirit, I rebuke every marine spirit and spiritual personality sent on assignment against my dream life. I nullify their influences, attacks, and manipulation in the name of Jesus Christ.
24. By the anointing of the Lord, I destroy every yoke of satanic and evil dreams that are holding my life and destiny hostage. I disconnect myself from every effect of such yokes now and forever in the mighty name of Jesus.

25. I release the fire of God to burn into ashes, every evil covering which the devil is using to cover my blessings through evil dreams in Jesus's name.
26. Every evil and satanic arrows sent or fired at me in dreams, I render you powerless now, and I return you back to the sender in Jesus's name.
27. I regain and recover by fire my financial blessings, my spiritual blessings, my material blessings, and my health now in Jesus's name.
28. I recover every of my money being spent in the dreams by demonic personalities through oppressive reverse representation, I recover them now in the mighty name of Jesus.
29. I recover my glory back now by the authority of the blood of Jesus.
30. I renounce and reject any name, symbol, or image which the enemy has assigned to my personality, which is been used by the enemy to link me in dreams.
31. I cover my personality, my names with the blood of Jesus, and I take authority over my personality my image or my names. I deny access to the enemy and bond them from manipulating my names for attack in dreams in Jesus's name.
32. I reject and command for total destruction of any personality using my names in dreams for evil agenda in Jesus's name.
33. By the power of the blood of Jesus, I reject any evil food introduced to me in dreams from now on in Jesus's name. I refuse to eat or swallow any evil food or drink given to me in dreams in Jesus's name.
34. I vomit and throw up every evil and satanic food or drink I have swallowed in dreams in the mighty name of Jesus Christ.
35. I confess that by the healing power of the Holy Spirit, I receive healing in all organs of my body of any disease, ailment, or medical condition caused by eating satanic foods in dreams.

36. I decree by the power of the blood of Jesus, I reject and rebuke every spirit of sexual perversion sent on assignment to me by the devil in Jesus's name.
37. I rebuke every power of the marine kingdom of spiritual sexual assault and spiritual control over my life in my dream in the mighty name of Jesus.
38. By the power of the Holy Ghost, I take authority over my sexual organs and my entire systems against every sexual manipulation in my dream in the name of Jesus.
39. I command total restoration and healing of any part of my sexual system that the enemy has attacked or oppressed by the power in the blood of Jesus.
40. I decree that my dream life will receive divine enablement for heavenly revelation in Jesus's name.

(viii) Scriptural declaration of victory through the blood of Jesus

Blood is ordinarily a mysterious substance. The very sight of blood brings to mind all kinds of serious connotations, especially as it is so intricately tied to life and death. In the history of creation, it is recorded that God formed man from dust. He had no life in him until God breathed upon him, and he became a living soul. Immediately the spirit came upon man, and blood started to carry his life.

> For the life of the flesh is in the blood. (Leviticus 17:11)

Now if blood carries life, we can conclude that life's very essence is in the blood. The Bible records that when God was establishing His covenant with Noah and telling him what he could and could not eat, and he specifically warned him in *Genesis 9:4* against eating any meat that still had blood in it because *the life is in the blood.*

> But flesh with the life thereof, which is the blood thereof, shall ye not eat.

Speaking with specific reference to the blood of the Jesus, *Revelation 12:11* states,

> And they overcame him by the blood of the Lamb, and by the word of their testimony; and loved not their lives unto the death.

Truly, there is power in the blood. But many do not understand the magnitude of this power, neither do they really appreciate the implications of the shedding of the blood Jesus for the human race. In order to grasp the true essence of the overcoming power in the blood of Jesus, we only need to retrace God's divine plan in bringing the Savior to earth.

Prayer points

1. "Through the blood of Jesus, I am redeemed out of the hand of the devil" *(Ephesians 1:7)*.
2. "Through the blood of Jesus, all my sins are forgiven" *(Psalm 107:2)*.
3. "The blood of Jesus, God's Son, continually cleanses me from all sin" *(1 John 1:7)*.
4. "Through the blood of Jesus, I am justified, made righteous, *just as if I'd* never sinned" *(Romans 5:9)*.
5. "Through the blood of Jesus, I am sanctified, made holy, and set apart unto God" *(Hebrews 13:12)*.
6. "My body is the temple of the Holy Spirit, redeemed and cleansed by the blood of Jesus" *(1 Corinthians 6:19–20)*.
7. "Satan has no place in or power over me through the blood of Jesus and the Word of God" *(Revelation 12:11)*.
8. "In Him (Jesus), we have redemption (deliverance and salvation) through His blood, the remission (forgiveness) of our offences (shortcomings and trespasses) in accordance with the riches and the generosity of His gracious favor, which He lavished upon us with every kind of wisdom and

understanding (practical insight and prudence)" *(Ephesians 1:7–8)*.
9. "Let the redeemed of the Lord say so, whom He has delivered from the hand of the adversary" *(Psalm 107:2)*.
10. "But if we are (really) walking and living in the light as He (Himself) is the light, we have (true) unbroken fellowship with one another and the blood of Jesus Christ, His Son, cleanses (removes) us from all guilt and sin (keeps us clean from sin in all of its forms and manifestations)" *(1 John 1:7)*.
11. "Therefore, since we are now justified (acquitted, made righteous and brought into a right relationship with God) by Christ's blood, how much more (certain) shall we be saved by Him from the indignation and wrath of God" *(Romans 5:9)*.
12. "Therefore, Jesus also suffered and died outside the (city's) gate in order that He might purify and consecrate (sanctify) the people through (the shedding of) His own blood and set them apart as holy (unto God)" *(Hebrews 13:12)*.
13. "Do you not know that your body is the temple (the very sanctuary) of the Holy Spirit Who lives with you, Whom you have received (as a Gift) from God? You are not your own" *(1 Corinthians 6:19)*.
14. "You were bought with a price (purchased with preciousness and paid for, made His own). So then, honor (your) God and bring glory to Him in your body" *(1 Corinthians 6:20)*.
15. "And they have overcome (conquered) him by means of the blood of the Lamb and by the utterance of their testimony, for they did not love or cling to life even when faced with death (holding their lives cheap till they had to die for their witnessing)" *(Revelation 12:11)*.
16. In the name of Jesus, O Lord, baptize me with the fire of deliverance in the name of Jesus!

17. All demonic spirits attached to all covenants and curses, I bind you and command you to come out of my life in the name of Jesus!
18. Father, let the blood of Jesus Christ erase all my sins that opened the doors to the curses recorded in the Bible in the name of Jesus!
19. By the power of resurrection, I reverse every negative decree already signed against me and that can affect me in any form in the name of Jesus!
20. Father, reverse every negative order placed over my destiny in the name of Jesus!
21. Holy Spirit, let Your voice respond on my behalf wherever my name is written or mentioned in the name of Jesus!
22. Holy Spirit, confuse my enemies in their own camp in the name of Jesus!
23. Let the power of God tear down everything the devil has put together concerning my name in the name of Jesus!
24. Under the new covenant that is the covenant of the blood of Jesus, I renounce all the evil works I have done in the lives of innocent people through my membership with these demonic associations, and I ask the Almighty God to forgive me and cleanse me with the blood of Jesus in the name of Jesus!
25. I request the blood of Jesus to flush out my system, purify my body, and cleanse me from all evil things I have eaten in any of the demonic cults or associations in the name of Jesus!
26. Wherever my name has been initiated either consciously or unconsciously, I withdraw and cancel my name from their registers with the blood of Jesus in the name of Jesus!
27. By the power in the blood of Jesus, I withdraw any part of my body or blood deposited on their evil altars in the name of Jesus!
28. I withdraw pictures, objects, presentations, food, sacrifices, money, children, wife, husband, clothes, images, and any

other personal belongings from the altars of the forces of darkness in the name of Jesus!
29. I return any weapon (physical or spiritual) belonging to the kingdom of darkness that I was a part of, and I also return any other properties for the execution of satanic duties at my disposal in the name of Jesus!
30. Holy Spirit, build a wall of fire around me and let there be a permanent disconnection between the satanic kingdom and me in the name of Jesus!
31. By the blood of Jesus, I cancel and erase every evil mark, incision, tattoo, and writing inserted on my body as a result of my participation with the forces of darkness in the name of Jesus!
32. I break all covenants that I have undertaken for my children, grandchildren, and generations after me in the name of Jesus!
33. By the power in the blood of Jesus, I renounce and denounce every dedication of my destiny to any river, mountain, or idol in the place of my birth in the name of Jesus!
34. By the power in the blood of Jesus, I renounce and denounce every initiation into occultism by my parents and/or grandparents in the name of Jesus!
35. By the power in the blood of Jesus, I cancel every dedication or covenant with family idols, evil trees, forests, markets, road junctions, and so on in the name of Jesus!
36. Anyone monitoring me through a satanic glass or device, I command that glass or device to be broken in the name of Jesus!

Now begin to thank and praise the Lord:

> Lord, I worship You. I empty myself and surrender my all to You, Lord. Come into my life, Lord Jesus, and fill me afresh. I give You my everything, Lord, in the mighty name of Jesus! Amen.

AUTHOR'S BIOGRAPHY

Rev. James A. Solomon is the President of Jesus People's Revival Ministries Inc., as well as the General Overseer and Senior Pastor of Jesus Family Chapel, with 38+ branches, in Nigeria, the United Kingdom and several other countries. The international headquarters for both ministries is based in Atlanta, Georgia, in the United States of America, where he currently resides.

Rev. Solomon is a man who is truly gifted with an extraordinary anointing on the subject of Spiritual Warfare, Healing and Deliverance. In his efforts to serve the body of Christ beyond his own ministries, he also serves as director for the West African Regional Directorate of the International Accelerated Missions (I.A.M.), a network of missionary churches based in New York.

Rev. Solomon started from very humble beginnings in his native country of Nigeria, West Africa, way back in the 1980s. With his team of ministers and due to popular demand, he has taken the revelation of Spiritual Warfare and Deliverance to massive venues such as the stadium domes in the major cities of Nigeria. He has also conducted a series of conferences, and organized quarterly Deliverance Night Services in the United Kingdom, Europe, Canada, Japan and all over the United States. Many have received freedom from satanic bondage and oppression at these quarterly deliverance services. He is in high demand as a guest minister in many crusades and conferences.

Milton Keynes UK
Ingram Content Group UK Ltd.
UKHW040020281124
3169UKWH00051B/100